PUBLISHED *by* PARABLES
Earthly Stories with a Heavenly Meaning

Christopher Miller

A Life Of Care

Christopher Miller

PUBLISHED by PARABLES
Earthly Stories with a Heavenly Meaning

Christopher Miller

A Life Of Care
Christopher Miller

Published By Parables
April, 2022

A Life Of Care

Christopher Miller

PUBLISHED by PARABLES
Earthly Stones with a Heavenly Meaning

Christopher Miller

Table of Contents

Introduction

A wheezing set of lungs competes with a breathing machine adjacent in the corner...

A set of hollowed eyes stares up at me with a last sense of direction; I clear my throat before speaking.

" Would you like a glass of water? "

Are you comfortable?

I received a snappy reply in return, "no I'm dying."

Shockingly, what if I told you this isn't a story but my occupation...

My name is Christopher Miller #114360 and a resident of the Colorado Department of Corrections. I'm a Medical Assistant working as an Offender Care Aide III (OCAIII), which is the equivalent of a Certified Nursing Assistant (CNA), without the official title. What is so unique about my job is that, I care for fellow inmates who are both terminally ill and dying sadly. Yes for all of you out there, the prison system does have its own hospital, It's called the "Infirmary". We take care of our own alongside with the dedicated nursing staff, twenty-four hours a day, seven days a week, pandemic or not. All of this care takes place at the Denver Reception and Diagnostic Center (D.R.D.C.). An OCA like myself only makes $2.40 per day, yes per day, not per hour. We care for patients just as if they are in a real hospital or long term care setting. The care we provide ranges from assisting with activities of daily living (ADL'S) to hospice end of life care. It's a humbling yet eye opening experience. My work in the Infirmary has awarded me many opportunities to learn valuable experiences that I can utilize upon my release. I'm passionate about patient care and what I do. I enjoy helping those that cannot help themselves.

"Because We're All Human"

Some People wonder...

why do I care?

why do I help?

why do I sit there listening to stories?

from a day and age when I wasn't even born

there when family's morn

that leave them torn

its like death is sworn

to break hearts

and make promises

leaving us with many questions unanswered

holding hands with dying men who find themselves

battling cancer

some people wonder

why do I care?

why do I help?

why do I sit there listening to stories?

"The Train Track"

I would like to take you all way back for a second. The year is 2010, my graduation year. I had just started my Externship. I was super excited, motivated, and anxious all at the same time. It was my first week and I was working in the county jail as a Medical Assistant, completing my externship requirements for graduation. So in other words I'm brand new, just stepped out of the classroom type of new. And for those of you out there who have been in this situation, you get my drift. Anyway one of my assignments on this night was to perform dressing changes. Now in case your asking the question, what is a dressing change? It is when you go in and properly clean the patients wound and change the whatever type of bandages may be in place, to prevent the wound from becoming infected. The deputies bring this patient back from the hospital who has somewhat recovered. So it being my first week and all, this particular patient had staples from the top of her chest all the way to lower part of her stomach. There were so many staples I literally lost count. I'm serious this woman was a train track. Now on this stormy night I was tasked to take out all of these staples. I have my Staple Remover in hand, I begin gently removing all of these staples one by one, thinking to myself "this is gonna take all night", "Its my first time", all the usual nervous excuses. But right in the middle of the procedure the freaking power goes out and my exam room literally went pitch black. All I could do was stand there and wait. Picture me, the newbie standing there with this tool in the pitch black trying not to move pulling staples out a woman's body. But seriously all I could do was stand there and wait because, I could've like accidently stabbed my patient or something. In that moment, I didn't freak out or burn a chip. I was calm, cool, and collective. It took about five or so minutes, but it felt like a lifetime for the power to finally come back on. During that whole entire fiasco, I kept my patient calm the whole time and completed the procedure. Years later I would discover that what I just experienced, prepares nurses to handle situations most people couldn't even fathom.

"My First Dead Body"

A few years ago when I first started my employment as an Offender Care Aide (OCA), that is what we as inmates are referred to as. But really were the same as Certified Nursing Assistants (CNA), just without the official title. Anyway I had my first experience with death. I got to see my first dead body. Better yet I was given the task of having to go the room and straighten out our patient who just passed away from cancer. I remember like it was yesterday, his eyes were still open like they were peering into my soul. He was oddly cold, I mean its to be expected when you die. The human body starts to go into what is known as rigor mortis, and the body starts to turn cold. Lastly, I remember him being kind of curled up on his side like he was avoiding something, something dreadful. Now with all of this in mind I go in and I gently and respectfully place him how he should look, at peace and with no worries of any kind. This experience can be a   make or break moment for anyone especially if your scared and timid of witnessing death and the stages that lead up to it. I can only speak for myself in this situation, but it made me a better Care Aide, and care giver by being able to care for my hospice patients in the present and in the future.

On another note this experience gave me the understanding I needed of what I truly signed up for...

"Prison Healthcare"

The frustrating part about being an inmate, well one of the parts because, there are many. The one particular subject that I want to share is about our medical care. Now I understand that being a ward of the state, we are not entitled to the "same exact" medical care as the normal citizens in the free society. Trust me I get and I'm not here to complain about it what so ever, or slander the correctional system but to enlighten everyone that our healthcare is a vital tool in our success and rehabilitation. I am a healthcare professional myself, and a ward of the state at the same time. Our medical care is less than substandard. The Department of Corrections is short on staff in every department including medical personal, i.e.; doctors, nurses, nursing assistants, pretty much everyone.

This is adding in budget cuts, no one wanting to come to work due to a crippling worldwide pandemic, all of this is affecting everyone in a negative way. It takes the inmate population forever to obtain medical appointments, I mean weeks sometimes. When we finally do manage to see a Physician, it's an uphill battle for some to receive medical treatment, "everything being cost effective". Please do not be misunderstood or misled we do have staff and medical staff that care deeply about our well-being, that treat us with the utmost care and compassion. It's not a people problem it's a policy issue, and these so called policies cause the majority of the outstanding medical staff to transfer within other state facilities, leave and go work in the hospitals, or just outright quit all together because, they outright lose the passion for patient care they came in with…

"I'm Not An Animal"

I'm not an animal…

I know the difference between the two

I am a human being

but I wonder sometimes…

are you?

they say

you can tell the way a person is

by the way you treat the people fairly

I mean when you fail to care for each other

in any state its embarrassing

is that too much to ask?

At times maybe it is

just like the men I see

and the things I can't forget

I guess we are all distend to see the truth

no matter how its revealed

I just know healthcare is equal to selfcare

so at times is my fate concealed?

"We Are Still In Prison"

I had the pleasure of working with a patient a couple of years ago. I'm going to refer to him as Xavier for obvious reasons. Xavier was sentenced to prison, but when he came to prison he was already a quadriplegic and he was sent directly to the to the Infirmary for our care. Xavier was a challenge to say the least, and I like challenges. At first meeting Xavier with his demanding personality and entitlement attitude, I actually enjoyed working with him and getting to know him. I performed his Range of Motion exercises with him everyday to help reduce his pain and prevent the splasticity in his muscles and joints, but most of all help reduce his pain. He has a long road ahead of him. Xavier couldn't do anything for himself, we had to feed him, bathe him, clothe him, and do everything to make his life more enjoyable. Now see here's the thing, we as inmates are considered "state property", that means our options are limited. We sometimes have to embrace the care we receive from our caregivers. Xavier was not understandably receptive to the care he received to the care he received at times. To highlight what I'm saying, myself and other OCA's gave him more one on one care and attention then he would have received in a residential care setting. You know the places I'm referring to its 1 CNA to 16 patient ratio. He still complained as if this was the

"Ritz Hotel". Now to get to my next point of this story, one day the powers at be decide to release him to a residential care facility until he paroles. Xavier manages to become argumentative and abrasive toward his care givers, I believe if I'm not mistaken he managed to even get into it with the actual "Pharmacist", you know the person whose only job is to account for pills. Now the officers who are guarding him have to bring him back to the prison Infirmary to finish out his time.

Now he's back in the personal hell he was desperately fighting so hard to get out of.

"Sometimes hell is in the mind and heaven is in the heart".

"The Addiction"

For my next story, I've decided to open up and share with the whole entire world is one of my very personal stories. Before my incarceration I was addicted to opioid pain medication and cocaine. This was a quiet and very lonely place in my life that lasted up until only a few years ago. Yes, I was one of those strung out healthcare professionals with a silent addiction. My addiction finally caught up with me after I had been up for a few days without any sleep what so ever, honestly, I was on a binder and I went back to work. I miscalculated a dosage for an injection I was supposed to administer on a patient, and I almost caused my patient to have a reaction. I could have caused serious harm to my patient that afternoon. Then to add fuel to the fire, I fell asleep in the restroom for like an hour all in the same day. The Physician I was employed for at this time summons me into her office, and proceeds to lecture me about being accurate, punctual, and how it is out of my character to make mistakes of such magnitude. She's questioning me about my lapse in judgement and things of such nature, I'm just sitting there like everything is kosher, well at least I thought it was, little did I know… I guess her intuition had somehow kicked in or she just flat out recognized the signs of my "self-destructive" behaviors. Whatever it was she saw in me call it my "true potential", she did not give up on me that fateful day and fire my behind on the spot. After another seeming like forever stern lecture about how I better never pull another stunt like this again. She sent me to a drug/alcohol rehabilitation program to get my what seemed like at the time felt like my worthless life back on track, and it worked well mostly, but not without those occasional slip-ups as we addicts would call it. The correct term being relapse. Hey what can I say no ones perfect and no one working any of the programs perfect. Sobriety is a day to day achievement and you truly have to want to stay that way. I'm not proud of the fact that I'm an addict, I just own it and embrace it. When the people around me found out I was an addict they panicked, the majority of the people I knew abandoned me and left me to deal with this alone. How do you think that turned out?

I weigh out the consequences of relapsing even now that I'm incarcerated and sober. When the temptation arises, I'm always thinking about the consequences of what I have to lose nowadays...

And nowadays I'm winning...

Christopher Miller

"Personal Hell"

Dark ally's and roads that break

parents that know heartache

lying to yourself in the mirror

telling your kids its ok

waiting in the snow

to break and bend so low

only to go

to an abandon state of mind

only to show

what you can't find

everyone sees all the signs

but they tell themselves never mind

its like they obligate me to get high

afraid to ask me why

I wanna die

running out of supply

and family ties

trading my self esteem

for what seems

to be destroying

I yell for but it seems

their ignoring me

maybe because I'm abandoning myself as well

my addiction

my excuse

my hell

"Cancer"

During these past few years I've had the unfortunate front row seat of witnessing cancer while working in the Infirmary. For my first example **Brain Cancer** or **Intracranial Tumor** if we want to get technical. I remember this woman vividly she used to scream half the night in agony. Oh and by the way we also have female inmates that are patients here too, seeing as how Denver Women's Correctional Facility(DWCF) is only 80ft away. DRDC is the only Infirmary in the entire state of Colorado to house female inmates with various terminal illnesses. When I met this young woman she was so attractive, but had that scared look of concern like her whole world just came crashing down. Turns out it did, Over the next couple of weeks I witnessed this young woman's brain cancer take over her body like nothing I've ever seen before. She lost all of her long pretty hair and went completely bald. She turned pale white like a ghost, and this disease stole all of her weight. The late night screams for help, pain medication only works up to a certain point. I work the graveyard shift, so for the most part everyone is asleep. I can hear all of this going on from my workstation. Sadly I've grown accustomed to hearing this type of sounds night after night. Fortunately for this beautiful young woman she was able to be released to live out the rest of her days gracefully with her family and love ones.

My second patient I assisted in taking care of suffered from **Bone Cancer**, the medical term pronounced **Osteosarcoma.** This is another awfully painful disease, I mean they are all painful diseases and I'm not trying to make any comparisons, but some are more painful than others. From my understanding bone cancer causes the individuals bones in the affected areas to become frail and can snap like a twig if you're not careful with your patient. This gentleman used to scream throughout the night in agony. I remember just being there trying to offer my morale support at times as he was crying out in pain. Everyone is administered pain medication, the highest dose possible to ease an individual's pain, and keep them comfortable. After awhile all they do is take the edge off, sad situation to say the least... As a care giver you wish you can make all the pain and suffering go away.... I was glad he was also released to his family to spend the rest of his days surrounded by love ones.

Not everyone is so fortunate, there are countless numbers of individuals that sadly die alone in prison from various terminal illnesses. Some inmates just do not have family at all, and the cold reality, there are some that have family they just don't care enough to come see them and spend time with their so called love one in their last moments of life on this earth. Part of our job as Offender Care Aides is to be there during an individual's last days, so that they do not have to die alone in prison.

Now the most common type of terminal illness that I'm used to seeing is **Liver Disease**, the correct term being **Hepatocellular Carcinoma.** Now unfortunately this nasty disease is usually brought on by the individual themselves due to the lifestyles they were living before incarceration. The examples I would like to present are, consuming mass quantities of alcohol, and sharing needles for intravenous drug usage. I could give more examples, but these are the common factors, and why bore you with a bunch of unimportant details. This type of disease is what I see most people die in prison from every year. These are usually the people that do not get released to go home and live out their days with their love ones by their side.

I once took care of a man who only had a two year sentence for Habitual Driving Under the Influence (DUI). He sadly passed away while serving his sentence in prison from stage IV Liver Disease.

Finally my the last but I'm sure not to be last terminal illness I had to witness was **Pancreatic Cancer**. The correct medical term being **Pancreatic Adenocarcinoma.** I cared for this patient for almost a year, I really got know him. Unfortunately he was not released to go home. He did however have family come in and spend time with him everyday and night until he passed. Having the privilege of getting to know this man on such a personal level made me both sad, but a stronger

Care Aide at the same time due to dealing with the harsh

realities of terminal illnesses and the outcomes they

produce.

"Do You Know Cancer"

I asked have you ever seen a soul leave a body?

traveling to a place unknown

so you sit there for a minute

all alone contemplating

what life has to offer

what it has shown

watching a grown man moan

or ask to go home

knowing it's not possible

just another spirit that roams

I ask

Have you held the hand of a dying man?

promising him to make unfulfilled plans

trying to get up and stand for something

but he doesn't understand

this is the end

I ask…

Do you know Cancer?

"C.P.R"

I remember the first time I performed C.P.R. one someone. Every Sunday evening I go over to my parent's house and do the dinner thing like normal. If I remember correctly we were having a beef roast or something. I never thought I would ever have to perform C.P.R. someone, I mean its in my training just one of those tools I thought I would never have to use. "Never say Never", mainly on the day to day patient care I specialized in at the time (Preventative Health) all I did was administer injections at an allergy clinic, for the most part all of my patients were predominantly healthy. On this summer evening I was wrapping up dinner, my father and I were out in the porch having a casual conversation. I was about to leave and go home, suddenly the neighbor's son comes bolting out of the house and he's screaming for help. I mean like someone's being murdered type of help. My father and I run over, he makes sure everything is safe. We then proceed inside the house to find my neighbor who was just released from the hospital for major surgery, on his bathroom floor in a pool of his own blood. On top of he's unconscious not breathing. Some how he slipped in the shower, tore his sutures, and bled out. There are some details I left out of this story for obvious reasons, I'm giving a run down of the situation. Without second guessing the situation my instinct and training kicked in, I went to work on him. His wife who was also a retired nurse worked to stop the bleeding. I started doing chest compressions 30 & 2 that's thirty chest compressions and two breaths. While my father stayed on the phone with the 911 operator and what seemed like forever, but was only like ten minutes, the paramedics arrived to take over. By some miracle he survived that evening. I went and visited him a few days later, he thanked me for saving his life.

"Covid"

2020 that year rained nothing but lemons. Statewide covid lockdowns, visitations NO…

Nothing, everything a complete standstill… The world as a whole now an unknown. A worldwide pandemic, what are the odds of that? I'm still asking myself this question; never thought I would see a pandemic during my time on this earth. Across the state of Colorado one by one facilities went on lockdown due to rising covid infections, and just when everyone thought it was safe to come out, damn another positive case, everybody lockdown!!! 14 days… Then another and another so on and so forth. Every time one of us tested positive for covid the entire facility went back on lockdown. Most facilities stayed on lockdown for months at a time. Every facility has their own unique story to share, how it happened, who was infected, and how many people were infected. Sadly some inmates and staff passed away from this pandemic of biblical proportions. 2020 was a roller coaster of a year not just for myself, but the inmate population as a whole. I must add on a positive note; The Denver Complex did not suffer no where near as many covid infections as other facilities across the state of Colorado. This was due to the strategic planning of the management team. I am considered an essential worker, and being in that role every time there was a positive covid case myself and a select group of OCA'S were assigned to move up into the Infirmary to perform our job duties, taking care of our Special Medical Needs Patients, and assisting the nursing staff twenty four hours a day, seven days a week. Our select group of OCA's stepped up and did this not just once, not twice, but three times over a year period to assist our inside community.

Its not something we had to do, its what we wanted to do.

Since our facility is considered a medical facility we also

assisted taking in some of the covid infections from other

correctional facilities across the state, this was a diligent

effort to keep the open in the hospitals for the most

serious patients, and not overwhelm the healthcare

system. The Denver Complex remained on modified

lockdown for almost an entire year, actually it was a

year. Now for those of you out there that have never been

locked up, incarcerated, seen the inside of a cage,

whatever term you choose. A modified lockdown is a

type of lockdown where we are not just restricted to our

rooms/cells. Our movement is restricted somewhat

around the facility to prevent the possible spread of the

virus to other parts of the facility. Then of course we

have level 3 lockdown, meaning we are not going

anywhere. We are restricted to our rooms/cells, no movement, we are fed in or rooms, and everything is brought to us, kind of like room service in a way without the smile. That tool is only utilized when the virus becomes out of control, and it has to be contained. Now with approved vaccines and routine testing available to both the inmate population and the D.O.C. staff. The Denver Complex has returned to its regular operations. The inmate population is punching the clock again going back to work, regular job. The educational curriculum has returned to normal, GED, College classes, orientations, and recreation have all returned to normal not to mention visiting. Our same routines before the pandemic, except we can seem to lose that annoying mask or sense of entitlement.

"Vampire"

The challenge of finding a vein in someone's arm, leg, or maybe a foot depending on where you have to go. The deep veins those are the challenging ones, I enjoy them the most, one their the hardest to find and the hardest to stick. Stick means poke in the arm. **Phlebotomy** also called **Venipuncture Technician** has always been my favorite position. I enjoy drawing blood or being a vampire. This is a precise skill that not many people can perform. It requires patience and most of all accuracy. Not many people can stand the smell or the sight of blood let alone try and draw it. Only about three percent of the worlds total population can even perform such a task. My second job I was employed at a Plasma donation lab. All I did was draw blood all day long twelve hours a day, and I loved it. It's amazing how the **Plasmapheresis** procedure works. We would draw your blood, then spin all of the plasma out of it. The red blood is then returned back into you're to regenerate itself. The plasma is like the heart and soul of the blood, it can be utilized for various medications and medical treatments for people with everything from bleeding disorders such as anemia, to soldiers that get injured on the battlefield. The learning experiences from this job were endless and the memories I will always look back and enjoy in the years to come.

On another note this procedure can be accredited to Dr. Charles R. Drew M.D. who developed this technique in 1938. He is known as

"Father of the Blood Bank"…

"The Free Blood"

Drip, Drip, Drip
sometimes accidents have a way of leaving
a messy solution
I mean get over yourself
you and I have the same thing inside of us
but for some odd reason
you believe your blood is better than mine
like you have some fancy wine inner twined
in your veins
you see blood and we think pain
I see blood and think wow veins
keeping people alive like highways traveling to
remote locations
all doing the same thing
only arguing if its blue or red
like the politician said I'm not like you
and you aren't like me
we don't have the same blood
home of the land
home of the brave
home of the free

"The Rant"

In this next all but true story, I want to talk about or more like rant about a certain type of inmate/patients. These are the type of patients that seem to have this false attitude that the care out there is better than what they will receive in the Infirmary. Now in some aspects the care out there is better, the food of course tastes better, you can move freely about, everything "appears nicer on the surface". In all reality the sacrifice is that, you're not going to receive the same "one on one" care out there in a residential care facility, that you would in here. The main reason for this and technically the only reason I need to present is that, in a residential care facility the just do not have enough care givers to go around. The ratio in a residential care facility is like 1/12 that's one CNA to twelve patients, some facilities even more. The Infirmary its usually 1/3 sometimes 1/4, and we usually have plenty of care givers to go around. We only make $2.40 per day, yes that's per day not per hour. I do this job because I'm passionate and I love my work.

If I had a nickel for every time one of our patients made the statement "if only I could get to the street, I could get better care". Sadly most of the individuals who are released from prison on medical parole die due to lack of care, and not having a care giver available to them at their disposal. The majority of these individuals lacked the resources they desperately needed to take care of themselves, example one on one care. The vast majority of these individuals complained, moaned, cried, fought with us, and tried every trick in the book to get released early on medical parole from prison. Now when they were released everything went to well you know....

The mortality rate of someone being released on medical parole is about 85% probably higher now with the covid pandemic going on, like I expressed "no one on one care", no resources. We as caregivers try our best to explain these uncertainties to our patients throughout their incarceration up until their release. It's not an effort to scare our patients were just trying explain "logical reasoning". In all I can say is good luck...

Good luck to all those who think the grass is greener on the other side...

Or better yet is there even grass at all...

"The Topic"

I was invited to do an article in a university newsletter. I was asked to share my experiences on this topic… What was it like growing up in a bi racial household?

When I was asked this question, I laughed a little, I was caught off guard, Its not really something I think about often. In all seriousness I'm honored to share my experiences on this topic. I'm a malito which means black and white. Growing up this way had its challenges, but I wouldn't say that I'm traumatized or anything of the sort. One challenge I had to experience was having an identity crisis, that stimulated from what is considered either not being black enough to hang out with the "all black crowd", or not being white enough to hang with the "all white crowd". I have always been stuck in the middle, the "black crowd" has always accepted me. As

I've grown older, I do not just concentrate on one side of my ethnicity, I have learned to embrace both sides and become one. I do not have an identity crisis anymore. Back then as a child people used to stare at us like we were from "outta town", that part I had a hard time understanding. When I was young I did not know what prejudice was, inner racial marriages were still somewhat taboo even in the 80's especially black and white couples. As the years past the taboo I think just sort of went away, and now a day's there is no such thing as a pure race anymore.

Finally what would I like to see change?

We are all people, it needs to be less of a race thing, and we need to come together as a people thing.

"Immunotherapy"

I had this really awesome job. I was employed in an allergy clinic. What was unique about this job, well at least I thought this was unique. We administered allergy injections to patients, but not just any allergies. We specialized in environmental allergies, you know like the things around us we breath every day such as, dust, grass, pollen, trees, weeds, and things of the natural environment. What makes this type of specialty interesting is that, we custom design an allergy injection to a specific patients need. The proper term would be **Immunotherapy**. How this works procedure works is, when a patient comes to visit our practice we would test them for the most common environmental allergies in the state of Colorado that people are allergic to. Now please keep in mind these particular patients' allergies are so extreme they can barely step outside to retrieve the morning news paper without having an allergy attack. After completing a ten prong test we observe which allergens the patient reacts to, then narrow them down to the top five. We measure this by how strong their arm reacts to the prongs we placed on the intradermal part of the skin. Finally we would design an antigen for the patient starting with the strongest dose possible at the beginning. As the patient's body became used to the antigen we begin to tone down the dose over a year period. Every patient is different changing the dose and time period varies. The whole idea behind was to be able treat the patient's environmental allergies so that, they can live a normal healthy lifestyle. On another note what made this practice unique, we were contracted with primary care physicians all over the city and three other states. I never worked in the same clinic every day. I enjoyed getting my foot in the door on learning about immunotherapy and the different variations of it. All I can say is complex… I look back now on this learning experience yearning for more, ready to move to the next phase…

"The Workaholic"

I'm workaholic or I just care too much, maybe I enjoy my job, I don't see it as "work", maybe its everything combined. I work twelve hours a day, six day's a week. I start my shift at 4:00 pm – 4:00am the night shift, I begin my night by coming in and performing Range of Motion exercises on a couple of patients to help relieve their pain. The medical term is Restorative Therapy, this does not cure the patient but assists the patient in getting the muscles moving, circulation, and preventing spasticity. That basically all this means preventing the joints and muscles from further locking and stiffening up, due to lack of movement throughout the day. This is the favorite part of my day, due to I actually am able to witness improvement in my patient and help temporarily relieve their muscle stiffness and pain. The next stage of my night is feeding my patient who is a quadriplegic dinner, then a quick snack for myself, and on to my next patient for his Range of Motion exercises. Follow that by our patients that must be turned every two hours, and the small details in between that. Some nights are slower than others, oops better watch that "S" word yea slow… Just when you think your going to have one of those calm, cool, and collective nights, Nope Hell No… People falling out left and right, fights breaking out, everything that could go wrong goes wrong type of nights… Those are the nights when it seems like everyone is called to show up the paramedics, fire department, even the police, lol I'm surprised the National Guard hasn't showed up yet. I do have downtime throughout the night in between my rounds, usually I'm studying or trying to learn and observe a procedure, wanting to perfect my craft. Throughout the night I will assist the nursing staff with other patients such as, dressing changes, observing

medication distribution, blood draws/labs, and vital signs.

This gives me the opportunity to observe so that I can

refresh myself and stay on top of what I have learned.

Finally I finish up the night by completing my final

rounds, turning our patients, and checking on the little

details. Now its time for a few hours of rest then back at

it again...

"It Never Stops"

As if the daily grind

is filled with props

the world is always moving

the workaholic moves with it

shaking, grooving, moving, & improving

as if chasing the wind

whatever adds up

the most unimportant important person in the room

plagued with the gift of scurry

stepping over you

under you definitely over you

trying to get ahead

they really aren't bad people

but they definitely have a positive problem

its not my place to say

I work for a living today

did you

workaholic

"Samuel"

The man that kept going to the hospital… It's a real thing, sometimes people prefer to not live in the Infirmary. Actually truthfully, they feel as if the hospital will treat them better. I have known this man for a long time, we were incarcerated together at another facility, and now due to unforeseen circumstances with his health he is now residing in the Infirmary in our care. I have personally been caring for him over the past two maybe three years now, its honestly been a privilege and a challenge. His name is Samuel, he has understandably developed this attitude that he just doesn't want to be in prison anymore. Now a day's he prefers to serve his time in a hospital setting with the regular upstanding people of society. Now I personally do not see this as a problem except, for all of the non-sense everyone is put through before he goes. It's funny because, we all see it every time like clockwork. On a serious note I understand the liability and what if there was something truly wrong with him? I ask myself, what more can I do for him? I feel sorry for him. Or what if he cannot bounce back from one of the "episodes"? I wish better for him. As I spend more time with him night after night, I cannot help but to sympathize with his situation. He feels there is no other way out. All I can do at this point is keep Samuel comfortable at this point is keep Samuel comfortable and to be his listening ear… Sadly Samuel passed away while OCA's were keeping him company one early morning…

Have you ever felt this way?

If you were in my shoes, what would you do?

"Thirty Plus"

Imagine for a moment that you have been incarcerated for thirty plus years of your life, you have been a quadriplegic the whole time. I had the pleasure of meeting such a gentleman almost five years ago, and I have been taking care of him ever since. Santos has been in prison almost longer than I have been living on this earth, and he's been a quadriplegic just as long. When I first Santos, well it was more like being thrown out to the wolves… I mean it wasn't quite that bad, but he was a little intimidating at first, and this arose from the fact he came with instructions. Not just with any instructions, they were very specific instructions, more like his own personal manual. He had to be rotated like this, his pillow fluffed a certain type of way, only four ice cubes in his cup of water, medication delivered on the timely hour,

54

type of instructions… (The Queen of England would be jealous). I had to learn all of this on my own with Santos instructing me on how to do all of his care. Not only was that a challenge to say the least, it was an experience. The Santos experience… He is very particular about his care, demanding about his needs, and expects nothing but punctuality on your part. Now to an individual who is not open minded you would be quite offended about these expectations, but over the years I have come to truly understand why he sets these rigorous expectations. It's not just due to the fact that he's "picky or spoiled". I realized that these rigorous expectations have actually kept Santos alive believe it or not. A quadriplegic only has their voice to express themselves to tell someone how to care for them. Santos just wants to have his dignity and still be fresh like the rest of us. I enjoy caring for

Santos on a daily basis, he actually sets the standard of how someone should be cared for.

The Santos Experience has developed me into a better caregiver by enhancing my listening skills and paying close attention to detail with my patients.

I ask

What would be your expectations?

"Paralyzed"

Don't move

don't move

or your legs

just lay there

barley able to turn your head

get fed by strangers

constantly live your life in danger

but don't move

a lack of control

makes you lose the thing you love

and the things you can't hold

thirty years served

damaged nerves

forgetting the things you heard

imagine if it was you with nothing to say

nothing to prove

but first and foremost

don't move

"Pediatrics"

While I was attending school, I had the opportunity to extend my studies somewhat and observe at a pediatric clinic. Now keep in mind at this time I did not have a child of my own, I had no Idea what to expect. Boy was I in for a treat, the first time I observed umm can't even explain it, and yes, I went back. I enjoyed working with the kids. At first, I did not have the slightest clue how my experience would turn out. I imagined chaos, confusion, crying and screaming children everywhere, with their parents trying to gather them up in orderly fashion. Like I expressed just expressed the first time, I didn't have any children of my own, I was trying to process all of this in my mind… My experience was nothing like that at all, shockingly the kiddos I had the privilege to work with that day actually enjoyed my company. I try to put myself in the shoes of a child, walking into some

unknown doctor's office, and not really understanding

why do I have to take this medication? Or why is the

person in this

 "white coat" poking, touching, and asking me questions?

I think the worst one, why do I have to get this shot? The

hardest part of that day was observing the other M.A.s

(Medical Assistants), no matter how great they were at

their job still, was administer injections. Watching the

kids especially the infants cry with that look of

misunderstanding on their little faces, you know the look

that I'm referring to, the one with their lip poked out and

the tear in their eye. You have to buy them ice cream

after that. Well even after that exciting experience, my

instructor invited me back to observe. Now this instructor

I am speaking of, he is the one who instructs my classes

at night. His name is Jeff, Jeff is the head R.N.

(Registered Nurse) of the pediatric clinic during the day. Jeff mentored and taught me what it takes to be a Medical Assistant, with that twist of a drill instructor mixed all together. Jeff served in the military and took me under his wing to try and keep me out of trouble. I was taught the fundamentals of healthcare, he taught me just about everything he knew, the tools I would need out in the field. While I had my crash course in pediatrics I learned how to do patient assessments on kids, vital signs, administer injections, calculate dosages, learn patient education, and how to effectively communicate with parents on what is going on with their child. Finally I feel most important, I learned how to work with kids, these experiences prepared me for when I eventually had a daughter of my own a couple years later...

"M.S."

Multiple Sclerosis is also known by the medical term

Encephalomyelitis Disseminata. This is a

demyelinating disease that the insulting covers of nerve

cells in the brain and spinal cord are damaged. Also

called M.S. for short can cause physical, mental, and

sometimes psychiatric problems. There is no cure for

multiple sclerosis, the treatments try to improve function

after an attack and prevent new attacks. Physical therapy

is helpful with people's ability to function.

This brings me to my next patient; his name is Pedro. I

met Pedro a few years ago at another facility before I was

an OCA. Pedro and were not friends by any means. Life

is strange how it comes full circle. Here I am employed

as an OCA for a couple of years and who do I look up

and see, Pedro… He's being wheeled in by a couple of

nurses. When he finally gets settled in, I have an

opportunity to spend time with him, see how he's been, and he tells me he has been diagnosed with M.S... I tell him if he need anything to let me know, as time goes by I figure out a way to help him. I start working with him and doing Range of Motion exercises on him everyday to help relieve his pain and get his body moving. I have been working with Pedro for about eight months and we have been able to gain improvement in his mobility. Some days are better than others M.S. causes flair ups and his joints & muscles will be stiff one day and loose the next. All we do is keep working and stay optimistic. Pedro and I have become friends from this experience, like I said full circle.

Sometimes your enemies become your friends...

In conclusion all of these experiences came together and made me a better Caregiver. I know some may read this and think I squandered opportunities in some aspects yes, I did. These were all teaching moments and some of them I had to learn from the school of "hard knocks". In all reality I have gained more opportunity, have had my true potential challenged, and had to expand my mind more than I ever would have in regular society…

Acknowledgments

I would like to thank the following people who played an instrumental role in my journey... Mr. William S. Graham a brother, friend who believes in me, and who challenges me to be at my full potential. My parents Bobbie & Cynthia Miller for always being there and doing there best by me. Bobby Miller my brother who shows me tough love when needed. My daughter Annabelle, the beauty in my life. Bethany Neal for being a positive role model and encouraging me to pursue my goals. Heather Basse for your support and encouraging me to want better out of life. Lastly Desiree Miller, thank you for making me feel something words cannot describe. I will always be here no matter what.

Thank you to all the Denver Complex staff in Denver, CO for supporting my positive endeavors.

Thank you to all the Medical staff for teaching me the fundamentals of patient care and strengthening my skills.

Executive Director Dean Williams thank you for your continued efforts toward humanizing the culture of the CDOC system and prison reform.

Governor Jarod Polis thank you for your ongoing support with criminal justice & prison reform.

www.ingramcontent.com/pod-product-compliance
Lightning Source LLC
Chambersburg PA
CBHW070938120626
46546CB00004B/1455